PEOPLE

. . . ARE

JUST DESSERTS

Experience the Sweet Rewards!

Written by
Your Hostess
Perry A~

PEOPLE

... ARE JUST DESSERTS

Experience the Sweet Rewards!

To Charlene~
a delicious
morsel of
rich fun~
from your
friend + mine
Ron Nielsen~
Sweet Rewards~
Perry A~
3/96

A Life Embracing Experience Created by:

Perry A~

Fifth Edition
Printed in the United States of America

Perry Productions

P.O. Box 33512
Austin, Texas 78764-9998

1-800-50-Sweet
(512) 441-0335
FAX (512) 441-0206

Printing History
First Edition - June, 1994
Second Edition - August, 1994
Third Edition - October, 1994
Fourth Edition - May, 1995
Fifth Edition - November, 1995

This book is manufactured in the United States of America
Written by Perry Arledge
Illustrations by Lisa-Elizabeth Berg
Cover Illustration by David Smith
Typesetting by David Nielsen
Editing by Marilyn Steele

Library of Congress Card Catalog Number: Applied
Arledge, Perry
People Are Just Desserts
ISBN: 1-887879-00-5

~DEDICATION~

For three years during World War II, my father, E. I. (Tommy) Thompson, published a newsletter called "The Newswheel". It's purpose was to assist our servicemen and their families in maintaining family ties in spite of the conditions that had been created in their world. He published letters from friends and family members as well as short stories and humorous bits and pieces. His heartfelt effort and the joy this small publication delivered to so many thousands of lives, instilled in me the belief that one person can make a difference in the world. Drawing from the many lessons and values he so generously brought into my life, I joyously dedicate this book to the memory of my father. I am reminded of something my father said while reflecting on the time he was publishing his newsletter, "It was hard work at times, but it was the kind of work you get a tremendous kick out of, and much more fun than fun." This simple statement sums up my feelings for this work ~ *more fun than fun.* And in keeping with this thought, this book is intended to be FUN! I encourage each reader to lighten up about life, and to begin to experience the Sweet Rewards that are available to each of us. If you will fully open up to what you find in this book, it could turn into a truly magical experience and you may find yourself having your own daily "Celebration of Life"!

Always remember . . .
Angels can fly because they take themselves lightly!

Perry A~
Austin, Texas
August, 1995

Your
Sweet
Rewards!

~Introduction~

We reveal our true identities in more ways than we realize. As a speaker, and chairman of hospitality for a speakers association, and being the unique and creative creature I am, I am always on the look-out for introductory topics which reveal information about the human *being*, not the human *doing*. Titles and business names are clearly visible on name tags and business cards - but what boring stuff! What kinds of things about people give us clues to reveal the true identity and personality beneath the mirage of the human doing?

A list of fun topics came to my mind, but I think none so vividly and accurately captures the true nature of the human being as what is revealed through dessert revelations. After I began developing and using the "People are Just Desserts Techniques" for several months, I discovered new, fun and exciting facets about people I thought I knew well. I began by asking virtually everyone I met the simple question, "If you were a dessert, what would you be?" I found through their selection of a dessert, several characteristics about the dessert closely matched the characteristics of the person himself. I soon realized this was a tool whose application had greater potential than had I originally anticipated.

Gradually more purpose emerged like rising cream on fresh raw milk. Not only could the question help one discover the true identity of a person which is all too often hidden beneath the glazed outer facade, it also could create an area of acceptance of our individual differences when we can look at each other as *Just Desserts*.

I had the opportunity, while substitute teaching various classes and ages of students, to practice the technique. I found it stimulated the students to try to discover special qualities in each other and it helped them understand and appreciate their own different characteristics as well.

Throughout this book, it is my intention to share some of these things I have learned about people and to show the reader, using analogies, to compare people's personalities and lifestyles to desserts. Although written with humor and with the intention of being fun, the underlying thought is that we are not really different from each other. I believe that our separation from each other is an illusion. I hope to create a desire in each person to embrace all of life's beautiful gifts and to connect with each other.

The technique of reading people's characteristics and human beingness and this book was born from my desire to foster a better world through understanding and acceptance of one another. This technique has been successfully demonstrated in schools, at work, in several health care organizations, in family situations, in recovery programs and in personal development trainings. I have used this method as an icebreaker after I have been introduced to people at banquets and formal dinners. It gets people talking to each other no matter what the occasion - and they have fun doing it!

I hope you, will find as I did, when you use the Just Desserts Technique, that there is beauty in recognizing and accepting people in all their uniqueness. This creates an opportunity for unconditional acceptance of who and what we are. You may find yourself experiencing a higher level of love for others and oneself. At any rate, it is my desire that you will have fun with it.

WELCOME TO THE WORLD OF JUST DESSERTS

Just Desserts, is a pathway to harmony. What if you could see ALL people in your life as Just a delicious Dessert? What if you knew each was calorie-free and had Sweet Rewards just for you? What if each offered only pure goodness?

Welcome to the World of JUST DESSERTS where all people are perfect and are just where they need to be, given the ingredients in their bowl. We are all working on our own dessert and with the ingredients we each have acquired, we're right where we need to be in our own development. Our job then is to learn to accept that each one is different and therefore has different needs, values, and opinions.

It stands to reason that you can't make Vanilla Pudding out of Chocolate Cake mix. Right? When we make an effort to see people without labels of right/wrong, good/bad, better/best, we can see them as perfect for the recipe they are creating. Then we can accept that their recipes are DIFFERENT from the one you are working on and let that be okay!

To help them best, master your own dessert, add creative swirls and garnish. Reflect for them HOW to be more. Allow them to observe you mastering your own ingredients. They will "get it" when they are ready. They will see it for themselves quicker if it is not pushed down their throats. Eliminate resistance by not being critical. Acceptance and self honor are the keys.

Create a balanced dessert smorgasbord by combining our different desserts to offer more. Add variety and spice by blending in harmony to be more than any one of you.

Perry A~'s Recipe for Sweet Rewards

1 Cup Acceptance (Self and Others)
1 Cup Understanding (That we are all different and perfect.)
3 Cups Honor Yourself. (Position yourself for your highest good in order to perfect your own dessert.)
Blend gently together for joyful results and 'Experience the Sweet Rewards' . . .

Let's look at these ingredients a little closer.

1. Acceptance: See people as delicious desserts. Accept that they are all they can be given their ingredients. Accept that they view life differently from you. Accept yourself as delicious and different also.

2. Understand: You cannot make Chocolate Cake from Vanilla Pudding mix. Understand that there is NOTHING right or wrong, first free will and choices as well as consequences based on each persons personal set of values. View other's opinions as different because of their life experiences and let that be okay.

3. Honor Yourself and the other person: Respect yourself, your needs and values. Without making the other person less than you, or right or wrong, evaluate how their position affects the results of the common goal which is -

acknowledge and validate their position. Position yourself to your highest good. Role model your values and state your needs. Create a safe, non-threatening space where they can be open to seeing things in a different way.

Blend for harmonious results. Ask how can we unite our separateness and our differences so that together we can become more than any one of us? Connection rather than rejection. Combine our strengths for a common goal.

When you have honored yourself and your own feelings with honesty and integrity, the universe moves to support you and a divine flow is created that makes life productive and happy.

By using the Just Dessert Technique to love and honor yourself as a magnificent and unique person, you will find a greater capacity to love and accept others just as they are. The greatest gift life has to offer is to be able to love one another unconditionally. Allow yourself to accept and embrace each others differences and let your own individual strengths support one another. Go ahead, S-T-R-E-T-C-H! Open your life to the possibility of experiencing the Sweet Rewards on the Dessert Cart in your life. Open your life to the full Menu that is available to each of us.

The MENU

Part One:

Calorie Free Fun!

- Experience The Sweet Rewards
- How to Use Just Desserts
- Identifying the Sweets
- Tasting the Goodness

EXPERIENCING THE SWEET REWARDS

Experience the Sweet Rewards of People Are Just Desserts, a non-threatening approach to seeing and accepting all people in your life as delicious morsels. How sweet the world can be if we can accept people and find their Sweet Rewards.

Think about this for a minute . . . what if . . . you knew that every person had a Sweet Reward just for you. What if together you could blend your special ingredients to create a delicious treat and make the world a better place. Would it be easier to create a harmonious bond if you knew the results would be delicious?

To Each His Own!

We cannot learn the lessons life brings for other people. Each person enrolls in their own class. Each dessert is different and in a different stage of development. Given our different stages of development we see life differently. The primary professor for the course is the *Big Chef in the Sky*. He uses us as role models to demonstrate our lessons for one another. We can only master our own ingredients. We cannot change or alter the ingredients in another person's bowl. We serve best when we stay in our own kitchen and master our own Sweet Dessert.

Life is about connection. Is the direction you are pursuing serving to connect or separate? Are you living your own life purpose? Are you positioning yourself to your highest good?

An unknown author captured the meaning in this poem:

BUILD A BETTER WORLD

And God said, "Build a better world." And I said, "How?"
The world is such a cold dark place. It's so complicated now.
And I'm so young and helpless. Lord, there's not much I can do."
And God in all His wisdom said,
"Just build a better you."

Unlikely Teachers in Unlikely Places

I have never met a person that didn't teach me something. Sometimes I see it as a positive trait I want to emulate and sometimes I see it as a negative one I want to avoid. Nevertheless, each person was their own unique dessert. I find now that I am eager to meet all people to see what Sweet Treat they have for me. I merely stay open and centered in my own values and observe. In this way I always find a Sweet Reward.

You will find unlikely teachers in unlikely places. Some of my greatest teachers have been students at the Alternative Learning Center. These students come for special classes on improving social skills. I remember one day, a particular lesson I learned as we were lining up the students to walk them to the buses, one of the students ducked into the crowd and ran ahead. I followed him and took him off the bus. He was made to go to the office to call his mother to come get him. He wasn't allowed to ride because he chose to consider the teacher's instruction as unimportant and to make his own rules. He had to pay a price for his choice.

He became angry and sat glaring at me, fighting back tears. I sat down with him and told him to take a minute to breathe and feel all the emotions that were coming up for him. When he had regained his composure and I felt he could hear me, I said, "Jimmy, what if you knew that your teachers knew something that you didn't know. That their instructions would be beneficial to your highest good. Could you not follow directions if you knew they were for your safety and well-being?" He rolled his eyes and sighed. Then I told him that we had been informed that because of the fight on the way to the buses the day before, that the city police were going to be on campus in case any gang retaliation broke out. That is why the sixth grade teachers had decided to walk their classes to the buses that day. It was for their safety.

About that time my mind said, "Like God has a plan for us that sometimes we can't see. Could you just trust that there is something planned for your highest good?" I had been resisting life calling me to this teaching assignment. I wanted to be writing, speaking and promoting my book. I suddenly got it, as I lectured him, that maybe God had a plan for me that I wasn't seeing clearly. I changed my attitude about my role as a teacher and found a perfect arena to practice the principles of my book. I was in the world's greatest arena of "right/wrong" thinkers. What an opportunity to teach them another alternative to fighting.

In addition, as I recognized the students acting out different roles like "procrastination, raging, manipulation, avoidance, and the 'do-it-my-way' syndrome," I was able to be aware of some of my own re-occurring behaviors. Unlikely teachers in unlikely places. They are all around us. The ones we criticize and judge the most have the biggest rewards for us.

How sweet it is savoring People as Just Desserts. Every person and every situation you encounter has a Sweet Reward just for me and for each of you when you are open to seeing it. I hope the Just Desserts Technique will help you begin to discover the deeper purposes in all your relationships and thereafter you will experience many Sweet Rewards. May Just Desserts serve as a pathway to harmony in your life.

How To Use Just Desserts

I have found that playing the Just Desserts game helped me identify true abilities in people and also revealed some of their preferences in life as well. Many people who have tried this technique have compared it to the Myers-Briggs Type Index (MBTI) which reveals personality traits and individual tendencies. These people say the Just Dessert Technique is similar and is <u>much more fun!</u> It allows us to get to know others in a good natured, light hearted and non-evasive fashion.

Let the games begin!

All you do is ask one simple question:

"If you were a dessert, what would you be?"

After having the answer, you visualize what kinds of characteristics the dessert has (i.e., smooth, rough, etc.) and begin to translate that information. Fascinate people by seeing their strengths revealed in the desserts they choose.

Go ahead, give your own dessert a try!

Ask yourself the question! "If I were a dessert, what would I be?" Now take a look in the index to find your dessert and read all about yourself...

I can just see you sitting there with your mouth open... Don't be so surprised! It was a shock to me when I first began using the technique a couple of years ago. It just works, and I have no scientific explanation as to why it does, nor have I taken the time or expense to do a "this or that" study. Why should I need to, it simply works. Now that you know that it works, you are ready to go into training to take your gift on the road and share the fun with others!

Just Desserts is an association/analogy game. Those of you who chose to play in the game will be able to verify the accuracy after you've played it a few times. I have used this technique enough to determine it is extremely accurate when people respond with the first answer that comes to mind. Their answer doesn't have to make sense or be logical. The first thought that comes is the one from the heart; it's the response that tells the story !

If by some chance the person you are playing with indicates that you are way off base in your analysis, ask the following questions. "Did you tell me your *favorite* dessert or what kind of dessert you would *like* to be?" The question is not what you would like to be, or what is your favorite, but rather "what would you be." If there is any confusion, simply clarify and re-state the question.

Secondly, if you notice the person thinking too long before responding, they have slipped from their heart into their head. What you are looking for is their intuitive heart response! This tells the story... If you notice any hesitation, interrupt their thinking and ask, "What was the first dessert that came to mind?" In short, if they answer the question and do so from their heart, you find the analyses are amazingly accurate. I have found that some people who are more analytical and less spontaneous will be looking for an underlying motive in my question and resist giving their true answer. But even a wacky answer from anyone will reveal a need to be different and not follow the rules.

Suggestions on Where to Use Just Desserts

Family Reunions

See your relatives in a new light. Gain a healthier understanding of how they perceive others. Learn to recognize and appreciate their good points and overlook that one trait which always drives you crazy. Remember, they are Just Desserts and an Apple Pie will always be an Apple Pie!

The Dating Game

See the person instantly and recognize their character traits. Chocolate Cake People or Pie People are perfect with Pudding or Ice Cream People. Discover the art of interdependence in relationships. Learn to bridge the gaps in our differences and contribute to supporting one another in positive ways.

Criminal Justice

See beyond their exterior facades. Recognize behavior traits and be able to point out in a non-threatening way the games they are playing. Stay one step ahead of the manipulator or the actor. Hold the inside advantage.

Interviews

Quickly and accurately ascertain a potential employee's personality traits. This technique will give you their strong points in minutes. Eliminates mistakes in mismatching employees and positions.

In the Work Place

Deal effectively with your fellow workers or staff by determining their strengths and weaknesses. Pudding People are creative, spontaneous, multi-task people need to know the results you want and to be given the freedom to use their creativity. They need clarity in understanding instructions. Pie and Cake People are goal setters and result-oriented. They just want the facts and no fluff. All have Sweet Rewards when handled effectively.

Icebreakers

Eliminate the stiffness at parties in seconds by playing Just Desserts. People bond instantly and love the fun and games it stimulates. Eliminate boring "air-talk" at a banquet or luncheon table. Liven up your bridge or social gathering.

Teachers

Elementary teachers can evaluate students the first day of school in a fun way. Assign the question, "If you were a dessert, what would you be?" Then have the students write how they see themselves and why. Put their dessert choice on their name tags the first week of school. After they have picked a dessert this helps them break the ice with each other too. Then it is also a teaching tool for creative learning exercises on journaling or verbally expressing their choices in a group discussion. Or have them draw family members as their desserts. Do art assignments and collages. Use different forms of art to express their dessert choice. School counselors can identify personality traits for quick evaluations.

Random Acts of Kindness

The Sweet Rewards of showing appreciation by sending cheese cake is overwhelming. My mechanic, postman, maintenance man, printers and bank clerks have all received cheese cakes from me and boy, do I get Sweet Rewards!

Have you ever sent a special acknowledgment to someone while you are at a convention? Send a Cheesecake. One slice delivered to their room with a note saying "Meeting you was a delicious experience. Thanks for sharing your Sweet Rewards." You will make a favorable and lasting impression.

Dessert Party Suggestions!

Tired of stale banquet talk? Liven up your table with a quick round of "If you were a dessert..." You don't even have to analyze them to have fun. Just ask them why they see themselves as that dessert? It is enjoyable and fun for all. Everyone has the opportunity to connect and to feel a part of the whole.

Take your friends out for dessert then try this . . . For six people, order three different desserts. Have them cut into six pieces, verbally give them some of the character traits that go with the desserts, then pass the desserts and the fun around the table.

Hold a planning committee meeting and finish up with a round of Just Desserts. Not only will they appreciate you, they will be eager to serve on your committee the next time around!

Have a "Decorate Your Own Cup Cake Party" for little ones. They love the game and are quite creative. They will have some truly delightful answers as to why they selected their dessert. Listen to them giggle with delight. A child's laughter is contagious.

Keep It Light

I can't stress too strongly that there are no "right" or "wrong" answers in this game. This is actually about getting out of the right and wrong game and into the acceptance game. This is not a heavy game nor one full of judgments. Remember that making judgments reveals more about the judger than the judged! Allow every individual to be perfect for the place that they are in at this moment in life. Everyone has their own learning scale.

My mother always said, "The difference between a good cook and a bad cook is a pound of butter." Use pure ingredients only! Skeptics and doubters will ruin the pudding. Like a good soufflé the key to success with Just Desserts is in *keeping it light*.

What you see is what you get...

Every dessert has it own unique combination of ingredients. Based on all our experiences of a lifetime, we are who we are. Embracing all our ingredients, *as perfect*, for what we are cooking up in our lives, is the key to success and happiness. Changing the end result is possible and requires decisions to change some of our basic ingredients. No one else can successfully change your ingredients. We have to choose to do that ourselves.

For instance, Vanilla Pudding Mix is quite different from Chocolate Cake Mix. Learn to work with your own ingredients and stay out of other's people's kitchens. When we do this, then we are free to create our very own specialties and to combine our finished product with others to become that balanced smorgasbord table. Life begins to get easier and we begin to accomplish much more when we shift from "What can I do by myself?", to "What can we accomplish together?". Ice cream and cake, Jell-O and cookies, strawberries and whipped cream, Cherries Jubilee and Cheesecake....etc.

IDENTIFYING THE SWEETS

Here are some guidelines that will help you in recognizing dessert traits that run throughout the full dessert cart. Qualities and traits are listed by colors, details, flavors, shapes, structure, temperature, texture and even toppings. This general information will assist you in analyzing deserts which may not be listed in this book. As you become more comfortable with the process, you will find yourself cooking-up analogies so accurate you will amaze yourself.

~ Colors ~

Red: Denotes high energy and attracts others. Loves crowds and audiences.

Chocolate: Rich, dark, serious and non-revealing. Self-protective. Tenacious. An action person. Determined.

Pastels: Soothing and pleasing. Comforting.

Earth Tones: Centered and at peace. Content as is. Quiet and thoughtful.

White and Yellow: Reflective. A giver or teacher. Denotes a spiritual core.

Multi-Colored: High energy and likes variety. Creative and unlimited. A visionary.

Transparent: Open and honest. Clarity and integrity are strong values. What you see is what you get. Nothing hidden or held back.

~Details~

Generalized or Vague Descriptions: Vague about directions and may want to change their mind. Doesn't like to be boxed in. Avoids commitments that might be limiting. Reserves the right to change their mind.

Specific Descriptions: Good communicators. Knows exactly what they want and communicates it well. A detailed analytical person. Visual. A decision maker.

Combinations: A team player. Goes well with other things. Resourceful.

~ Flavors ~

Bitter Sweet: Leaves a lasting impression. Is influenced by the past. An analyzer. Self-protective.

Hot and Spicy: A professional agitator. Likes to stir up things and plant seeds for thought. A trail blazer. Creative and challenging.

Mild: Content as it. At peace. Doesn't need to make a splash and be noticed. Soothing. Steady. Dependable. A pleaser.

Sweet: Nurturing. Pleasing and soothing. A giver of energy and encouragement. A caretaker.

Tart: Witty and stimulating. Quick to respond. Speaks out. Plants seeds. Direct and to the point.

~ Structure ~

Multiple Layers of Different Ingredients, Unstructured: Attention seeker. Gregarious and outgoing. Like to be noticed. High energy and spontaneous. Action oriented. Desires attention. Values freedom. Fun lover and creative. A resourceful builder.

Single Layered: Content and at peace. Steady relater. Doesn't need attention or approval from others.

Tall and Structured: Layered and organized. A builder who lays a careful foundation first. Each layer has a purpose. Methodical. Precise. An achiever striving for excellence.

~ Temperatures ~

Cold: Stop! Don't get too close until I look you over. Self guarding. The analyzer. Usually warms up and changes shape with time.

Hot or Warm: Inviting. Luring like a warm fire. Test the temperature, you could get burned. Aggressive when hot.

~ Textures ~

Course with Lumpy Protrusions: An enticer. Planting seeds of curiosity about what is under the surface. Slightly contained fun. Not sure if it is Okay to come out to play. Likes to be invited.

Crisp or Hard Outer Crust: Self protective. Protects sensitive inner softness with a hard outer coating. Firm in belief.

Fluffy or Whipped: Light-hearted and fun loving. Doesn't take life too seriously. Has a sense of humor. Soft and moldable. Sensitive to criticism. Creative.

Jelled Consistency: Takes a soft stand. Consistent, Nurturing, Feelers. Rewarding. Flexible.

Soft and Free-Flowing: The creamy smoothness of a stroker or caretaker personality. Moldable and flexible. Spontaneous. Gets along well with everybody. Willing to change direction. Open and adaptable. Goes with the flow of life. A peacemaker.

Spongy and Porous: Open and absorbing. An achiever-seeker. Curious.

~ Toppings ~

Sauces or Fruit Toppings: Something extra. Goes the extra mile. Luring and attracting. Spontaneous.

Sprinkled on Toppings: Added attraction. Dares to be different. A sample of what is to come. Advertisement. Decorative. A trend creator.

Contrasting Toppings: Goes from one extreme to another. An adventurer who likes to experience all of life. Look for balance.

Dark over Light: Duty over desire. Discipline. Dedication. Shows serious side first. Self-contained.

Light over Dark: Fun side up. Reserves serious side.

White Creme or Fluffy Topping: Portraying lightness and fun. Reflective and sensitive. Positive and open. Look beneath for the hidden inner treasures and experiences.

~ SHAPES ~

Flat: Likes to stay with the familiar. Has created a safe place and content to abide there.

Multiple Shapes: A Duke's mixture. Likes variety. Demands change. Easily bored with out variety. Creative. Likes to mix and match ideas. Not satisfied with sameness.

Round: Rolls rather than plans but has certain limitations. Looks for other options. Open to seeing another way. Changes mind often.

Square: Self contained with self imposed boundaries. Stays within a set perimeter but will change directions if it corresponds to their purpose. Speaks up when you threaten their boundaries. Self disciplined.

Wedge or Triangular: Focused with one end result. A results orientated person. A planner...organized and on task. Determined and tenacious. Likes completion.

And always remember...
Desserts are designed to be sensual experiences.
Play in all the senses when making your interpretations!

TASTING THE GOODNESS

Kicking off the Training Wheels

Now that you know how it is done, you are ready for the experience! Just as with everything else in life, the difference between knowing about something, and fully experiencing that something, is as different as night and day. So, I will ask you a question... If you had a choice, would you rather read the Dessert Menu itself or would you choose to experience the savory goodness in every tasty morsel?

To experience your Sweet Rewards you first have to kick the training wheels off your life and decide you are worth the FUN and excitement life has to offer. If you choose to go for life and all that accompanies such an adventurous choice, please read on... And congratulations on your choice!

If you are feeling some resistance to really S-T-R-E-T-C-H-I-N-G and playing the Sweet Reward Game with other people, consider reading the Commitment Process in Part Three. It may help you get over this hurdle of resistance. But, before you move on, at least consider loosening the lug nuts on your training wheels a bit...

Working with couples and with rocky road relationships is a great joy in my life. Harmonizing relationships until the resonate with clarity is one of the Sweet Rewards we can all chose to experience. Combining different flavors and textures creates unique rewards. Chocolate Eclairs, Fruit Cakes and Strawberry Napoleon are a few examples. It takes experimenting with different combinations and serving what tastes good to you. Apple pie with chocolate sauce might not be an appealing combination.

When flavors are not in harmony you may need to re-position and try another combination altogether. When I can't change the situation I always ask, "How may I see this differently?" Then I ask myself, "How would a teacher like Jesus handle this situation?" The Litmus Test for my answer is will the results of my action be "connecting or separating?" When I create that harmonious combination, flavorful Sweet Rewards will always result.

Each person must choose what compliments their taste palates. When you follow the recipe, you will find that everything for you and for everyone else is in divine order. Only when we deny our true selves, or attempt to alter the recipe, do we find the Sweets have turned sour. Thus the secret to creating true harmony... Honor yourself and your partner as perfect just the way you both are. In that mix you will find that alignment of purpose, furthering of values and assisting to the needs of the other will flow like Vanilla Ice Cream over a slice of hot Apple Pie.

As simple as 1, 2, 3...

Interpreting dessert choices is as simple as 1, 2, 3... Once you have made your choice, visualize the dessert. Look at and feel the texture, form, structure, shape and color. Consider its consistency, whether it is simple or complex. Notice all its ingredients. Look for density, clarity, uniqueness, detail and arrangement. Take a moment to savor its aroma. What does the smell suggest? Finally taste it! Note its flavor or combination of flavors, how it feels on the palate, its temperature. Notice whether it stimulates or soothes... Fully notice the experience of eating the dessert.

That's all there is to it.

Step out and have more fun than fun with it!

PART TWO:

The Dessert Cart!

* Cake People
* Cookie People
* Fruit People
* Ice Cream People
* Pie People
* Pudding People
* Unique or Combination People
* Questionable

CAKE PEOPLE

Open, airy, absorbing...always learning and seeking answers. Inquisitive minds. Analyzers. Need to know WHY? Achievers. They stay within a framework and have self-defined boundaries. Structured. Planners. Self disciplined, dedicated and duty bound they don't have time for trivia when on a deadline. On task and goal oriented. They like completion. Competitive, self-driven and reliable. They get things done. They prioritize with ease and eliminate time wasting activities.

Cake people begin with the ending in mind and have a plan for each step along the way. Being decisions makers and leaders, they feel confident when they know what is happening. Give them the necessary facts and the bottom line. They are fast paced. Don't keep them waiting. When dealing with cake people communicate with clarity and purpose and leave out the fluff. They are private about their personal lives and tend to remain unemotional.

They like challenges and figuring out solutions. Sometimes this requires them to gather the facts and find a quite place to mind-map in solitude. They like their private space. When fun is their goal, look for a good time. They can play as hard as they work but don't mix the two with a goal in sight.

Cake People are so self disciplined and dedicated they can accomplish a goal with success even if it doesn't honor their desire. They may develop an ulcer but they will take home the all important blue ribbon to show for it. Imagine their potential when they are really about their bliss.

Cake People Affirmation:

I blend fun ingredients that joyfully rise to every occasion for sweet, flavorful results.

23

Angel Food Cake

Open, light and airy with a delightful sense of humor. Has form, shape, and structure. A high achiever. Definite boundaries yet flexible. Doesn't need to be center stage. A steady and loyal friend. Thrives on learning. A sponge to knowledge and growth potential. A listener; always open to new avenues and thoughts. Mixes well with others. Reflective; a natural teacher.

Boston Cream Pie

Creative and unique, this special blend is cautious on first meetings. The outer chocolate coating is a self-protective barrier. Beneath is a versatile, interesting, sensitive and compassionate person. A planner with attention to details and an eye for perfection. Open to learning and likes change. Dares to be different. Has well defined boundaries but has a soft spot in the center. Getting to know them is a rewarding experience. A thinker-feeler. A rare combination of sweet rewards.

Carrot Cake

Spicy and fun. Full of delightful surprises. Structured, achieving, unique and high energy. Creamy smooth and inviting on top. Look closely at this one. Underneath the smooth exterior are treasures galore. A friendship worth cultivating. Creative and resourceful; will experiment with the unusual and create something different. Adventuresome. Focused. Likes to complete projects.

Cheesecake (See Pie People)

Chocolate Fudge Brownie a la Mode

A command performer who likes to be recognized for accomplishments. An achiever who is focused and goal oriented. Competitive and likes to win. Very intense when on task. Self-disciplined and bold. A leader who uses the power of discernment. Open to experiencing extremes. Sees things black and white. Hides his serious nature beneath the light reflective vanilla ice cream. A cautious observer. A constant tug of war between duty and desire. Balances work and play. Lots of energy.

Chocolate Layer Cake

A serious nature that is intense and focused. Has definite goals and likes to accomplish them. Competitive. Stays with one task until completed. Doesn't like to have loose ends dangling. Has firm boundaries and likes to make decisions. Open to learning, curious. Structured, a high achiever. Balanced and poised. Likes to make a neat impression. They work as hard as they play but don't mix the two. Decisive and action oriented. No time to waste on emotional fluff. Gets things done. A leader.

Cup Cake with Sprinkles on Top

This elusive cup cake doesn't like to take a stand. A generalist who may want to change direction, they avoid long range commitments. The fact that they were not specific on flavor and icing choices shows a tendency to avoid being "fenced-in". An expert in one area with an inquisitive desire to learn more. A high achiever rising to the occasion. Cup cake people stand alone and have a need for solitude. The sprinkles on top are the fun side up. Inviting and playful on first encounter. Spongy but with honorable boundaries. Circular they are constantly looking for other options and are open to experimenting.

Fruit Cake

Nutty, jovial, spicy and full of energy and variety. Self contained yet bursting with energy. Works at control and self discipline. Loves variety and gets bored working on one thing. Has definite boundaries. Involved in lots of things. Changes mind often. Likes to try everything. A high energy person. Appears carefree and playful but has a serious side. Many talents and knows about everything. Wants to experience all of life.

German Chocolate Cake

Structured and on purpose. Likes completion and plans. Has well defined boundaries. Clarifies what they will and will not allow. Shows their playfulness on the outside. Nutty and fun. Can work and play. Likes to combine opposites. Will mix the unusual. Likes variety. Goes the extra mile. A striving achiever.

German Chocolate Cream Cheese Brownie

A detail person that is specific. Stays within self made boundaries. A team player, open to learning, but likes a definite plan of action. Holds things together. Teases with a sampling of extra goodies on top. Self disciplined and dedicated to a plan. Takes a stand and sticks to it. A real softy when you get to know them. A loyal friend. A seeker of knowledge.

Ginger Bread

Spicy and fun. A loyal friend. Content with moderate boundaries. Knowledge and learning are strong values. Organized and single focused. Consistent. Doesn't like change. A traditionalist. Unique. A flavor with a kick. Witty and sharp. A team player, goes well with ice cream or lemon sauce. Self imposed rules and guidelines.

Italian Cream Cake

Structured elegance. Dares to be different in an sophisticated way. Very organized. Proud and dignified. Light and reflective. Open to entertaining new ideas. Makes a lasting impression. Takes things smoothly and in stride. An analyzer-thinker. Makes cautious decisions and is usually right. Attracts and empowers. Cares about their appearance. A gracious hostess/host.

Lady Fingers

Spongy and absorbent this person loves reading and learning. Education is on going. Soft and gentle. A nurturing, caring, compassionate person. Has a unique shape with honorable boundaries. Consistent and content with who they are without the need to grandstand and attract others. A team player...moldable and works well with others. Prefers others to take the initiative and make decisions. Goes with the crowd.

Mississippi Mud Cake

Beneath the rich chocolate exterior lies hidden treasures not revealed on first glance. Don't over look this person from the outward appearances. They are full of delightful surprises. They secretly desire to be spontaneous and playful but follow self imposed boundaries. Ruled by a belief of duty over desire. Tend to put their desire last. A strong team player, they handle details well and are amazingly well structured. Learning and growth are key values. Fun is a strong value.

Mississippi Mud Cake Recipe

4 eggs	1 tsp. vanilla
2 c. sugar	1 c. shredded coconut
1 c. melted butter	2 c. chopped pecans
1 1/2 c. flour	1 (7 oz.) jar Marshmallow Creme
1/3 c. cocoa	

Cream sugar and eggs. Combine butter, flour, cocoa, vanilla, coconut and nuts. Combine the two mixtures. Mix well. Bake in a greased and floured 13x9x2 inch pan in a preheated 350 degree oven for 30 minutes or until cake tests done. Remove from oven and spread Marshmallow Creme over top of the cake. Frost while still warm.

Mississippi Mud Cake Frosting

1/2 c. butter, melted   4 c. powdered sugar
6 T. milk   2 c. chopped pecans
1/3 c. cocoa

Combine all ingredients and mix well with wire whisk. Spread carefully over Marshmallow Creme.

Pineapple Upside-Down Cake

Unique and a real sweet experience. A charmer who is sincere and giving. Goes the extra mile in giving. Likes variety. A planner with goals but open to changing them and going another direction. Listens to others. Cares about appearance. Poised. Dares to be different. Likes variety. A colorful dresser. Self disciplined. Will stick to their plan.

Strawberry Shortcake

The cheerleader. This person attracts attention and has fun. Tart and exciting, they stimulate others to join in the fun. Not the detailed, organized perfectionist, they are more spontaneous. Likes variety and change. Tends to get bored doing one thing. Doesn't like to make commitments too far in advance as something better may come along. Finds it hard to settle on a decision. The spongy cake base shows a curiosity for learning. A team player. A real encourager for others.

~ COOKIE PEOPLE ~

Round...Looks at other options. Has 360 degree vision. Goes in circles if not careful. Likes roots. Likes to stay put. Has a tendency to adhere when comfortable. Steady and sticks to a plan. Dedicated to a cause. Absorbs ideas but needs time to analyze them. Logical and methodical. A team player...gets along well with others. An anchor.

Stable and reliable, cookie people are not prone to hasty decisions. Give them time to think it over. Practical and logical they like to look at all the angles. The crisp outer boundaries will break or chip when forced. They tend to attract the outgoing, spontaneous, compassionate types to counter their crisp edges.

Once committed they will stick with a project to completion. Stability is their strength. Not easily swayed. Steady as a rock.

Cookie People Affirmation:

I pass my goodness to reach all with sweet rewards.

Chocolate Chip Cookie

Round but flat. Stays within set boundaries but looks around. Sticks to decisions. Stable and secure. Definite boundaries. The inside is filled with rich rewards
for those who penetrate the exterior
boundary. A real softy in the middle.
Mixes well with light, reflective spontaneous types.

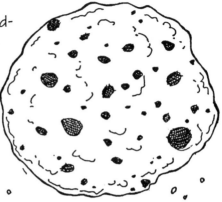

Fig Newton

An exception to the rule. Dares to be different in a subtle way. A dry sense
of humor, an enticer, and full of surprise. A bit of a tease with only a small portion of the fruity inside exposed.

The soft bland cookie dough
sets self defined bound-
aries. Inside a softy at
heart. The sweet fruity
inner portion is full of
seeds.   Plants
seeds of wisdom in
delightful surprising
ways. Stable, reliable
and fun to be around.

Oatmeal Cookie

More   than
meets the eye.
Involves others in
their activities.
Always   up   to
something . . . spicy
and   exciting.
Likes to have several
options available to choose

from. Tends to be self contained, but secretly bursting to get out. Attaches easily and sticks to a project until complete. Likes challenges, the rough and rugged type. Never boring. Full of surprises.

Oreo Cookie

Hidden between two crisp self defined layers is a rich and sweet reward for those lucky enough to gain this person's confidence. Serious and dedicated, a team player, structured, opinionated seeing only black and white. Doesn't veer from path. Sticks to the rules. Self disciplined and protective. Follows the path of Duty over Desire. When following desire can let loose and have big fun.

Sand Tart

Different with a unique shape and style. Unique. A natural teacher. The outer sweetness covers an inner dry wit. Nutty and fun. A creative innovator. Dares to be different.

Star Shaped Tea Cake

Unique, special but not fancy. Genuine. A crisp sense of humor. Definite goals and focused. A store-house of information. Content...at peace with self and others. A favorite. Works well with others. Has roots, not flighty.

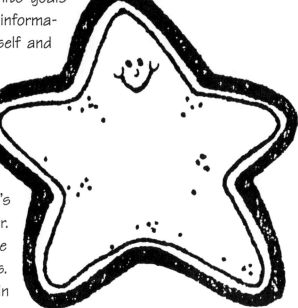

Vanilla Wafer

Round, crisp, absorptive. Nothing fancy but everyone's favorite. A great team player. Content with self. Dependable and reliable. Plain but delicious. Becomes soft when dipped in milk.

FRUIT PEOPLE

~ Fruit People ~

Juicy stimulators. Sweet-tart. Demand a response. Mind stimulator. Agitate and stir up thoughts and action. Mostly oval, rolls right along, outgoing and creative. Quick with words, thoughts and actions. Natural motivators, they empower and encourage others. Managers and leaders. People orientated. High energy and refreshing. Eager and high-geared, they often jump out of the starting gate without waiting for the starting bell.

To communicate effectively, create a quiet space out of the main stream of activity. Allow them to settle and ask for their undivided attention. Clarify your purpose in the beginning. Help them to focus with you.

They love the excitement of stress situations. It allows them to kick out of "think" gear and go into "respond" gear. Their juices really flow when they tune into intuitive feelings. They handle deadlines with glee.

Fruit People Affirmation:

Juicy, irresistible happiness and scrumptious joy are my delicious state of being.

A SPECIAL SWEET TREAT FOR FRUIT
Cinnamon-Peach Brandy Sauce for Fruit

1 cup sour cream (May substitute fat free.)
1 cup brown sugar
1 teaspoon cinnamon
2 tablespoons peach bandy
Mix well and serve with fresh fruit as a dip.

Anything Coconut

Does not like to make long range commitments. Wants to remain open to options. Flexible, easy going and agreeable. Pleasant and friendly. A team player that mixes well and likes change. Creative. Sweet tidbits of reward. Compassionate and caring.

Apple Sauce

Compassionate, caring, nurturing. A real giver. Satisfied with the basics. Doesn't feel the need to compete or achieve great recognition. Content to give and receive. Chooses not to lead and make major decisions. A team player willing to bend and go along with the majority. Doesn't hold grudges. Let's go easily. Fits any shape. Changeable. Spiced with a sense of humor.

Blueberry Cobbler

A fun lover. Spontaneous. Rolls along enjoying life. Not into long range planning and goal setting. Often changes opinion and choices. Not much into structure. Like to be free flowing and spontaneous. Tends to avoid conflict. Looks for other options. Open to changing perspective.

Ambrosia

Variety is the spice of life and this person demands variety. Multi-faceted and talented, they are into almost everything. Easily bored with just one project their minds are creatively at work developing new projects all the time. Change is ever present. Colorful, fun and full of energy. A team player. Spontaneous, creative and free flowing. Not rigid in plans they function on intuition. A performer, they like to be unique and different.

Blackberry Cobbler

This detail person is an expert in a specialized area. Loves learning new options and ideas. An achiever that likes the power of knowledge. Multifaceted. Thrives on mental challenges. Has rather soft boundaries and free flowing. Not much on structure and tends to lose track of time when involved on a project.

Cherries Jubilee

A stimulator lighting brief fires. Spontaneous, rolling in several directions at one time. Doesn't like limiting boundaries or committing to one direction. Creative and unique. Dares to be different. Works best when given a goal and allowed to be creative. A team player. High energy, attracts others, likes to be noticed. Thin skinned, sweet/tart and juicy. A mouth-watering, stimulating experience. The outer sweetness hides the inner seed or core strength. Sees from a 360 degree perspective. Always looking for another option.

Bananas Foster

A creative non-conformist. Strives on being unique and different. A catalyst who likes to stimulate others. Focused with moderate boundaries. Makes plans and goals but has a tendency to change direction. Sugar coated, emits energy and attracts attention with sudden bursts of fire. A people person. Sensitive, bruises easily.

Chocolate Covered Banana

Banana...soft, flavorful mushy. Bruises easily. On a definite path. Self contained by self impose perimeters. Chocolate coating is a protective boundary. Sees things as either black or white. Justifies a set standard. Will curve slightly but not prone to making drastic changes without cautious thought. Takes pride in being uniquely different.

Chocolate Covered Strawberry

A true enticer. Likes attention and attracts like a magnet, but then becomes closed or private. Issues an sweet invitation but without the magical password you are out in the cold. Tart and witty. A stimulator. Encourages people to respond. Appears smooth on the outside but many faceted on the inside. Single focused, organized and has it together. Has definite boundaries and opinions. Expressive. Somewhat focused but will roll. Be careful...they are addictive. Mouth watering.

Delicious Red Apple

Rolls along self confident and contained. Bright red...attracting. Semi-tough exterior, self protecting. Inside sweet juicy pulp, white and reflective. A natural teacher. A rewarding treat. Self disciplined. Spiral ...opened to all directions. Centered around a core. Strong belief system. Seeds of wisdom inside.

Kiwi Fruit

Definite stimulator. Sweet/tart. Oval and rolls. Has a double protective outer layer. A fuzzy hairy coating and tough-skin protect the juicy tender inner goodness. A star burst of flavor emitting from a center core radiating outward. Bruises easily. Content with who they are. An observer/thinker. Stay within a self impose boundary. Does not openly show the fruity inner beauty and goodness hidden within the plain exterior. Selective.

Peach Cobbler

Tart-sweet. A stimulator. Spicy and fun. Quick with a retort. Juicy and creative. Mushy...sensitive and compassionate. Bright and colorful. Tends to stir things up. Adds zest to life. Moldable. A team player. Likes to arrange things and handle details

Pineapple

A tough, self protective exterior hides a sweet juicy reward. Revolving around a hard core belief system, they radiate out in a circular pattern that has them constantly looking for new directions. Creative and challenging. Always seeking. Self contained, they stand alone. Strives for higher levels of achievement. You will want to devour the sweet juicy portion but take this tasty treat in small doses. It is highly acid. They demand respect.

Prune

Sweet but kind of dried up. Satisfied. Contemplators. Content with life. Just sits around and smiles. The tough exterior protects the sweet interior. The pit is central belief system. Strongly attached to beliefs.

Strawberries Romanoff (See Pudding People)

Raspberry

Red, the color of vitality and life. A high energy achiever. Attracts like a magnet. Focused and dedicated to a specific purpose. An expert, multi-faceted, in one specialized area. Sharp witted. Has a tartness that stimulates. Has definite boundaries but likes to look at new options. Will roll. A command performer.

~ ICE CREAM PEOPLE ~

Reserve and chilly on first meeting. Observers/analyzers. A real sweet treat when you are allowed into their inner goodness. Smooth and easy going. Gets along well with others, a team player. Must have people interaction. Moldable. Stackable. In a structured container they are organized, on purpose, balanced and fun. Changeable. Will go from a solid to a liquid given time to survey the situation. They have excellent listening skills.

Don't rush these sensitive thinkers. You won't pull any fast ones with them. They are cautious thinkers who land ideas first from the thought process and then from intuition. Patience develops trust and loyalty.

Ice Cream People Affirmation:

My life is creamy, smooth, cool, rich and delicious.

Ice Cream

A generalist who doesn't like long term commitments. Likes to be open to changing at the last minute. Reserved and chilly at first meeting. An observer/analyzer. After finding safety, real treats are in store. Spontaneous and fun loving. A real sweet treat. Smooth and satisfying. A great team player. Interacts well with all types. Moldable. Stackable. Will change positions easily.

Banana Split

High energy person likes the limelight. Multi-tasked. Has many activities going in various stages of completion. Thrives on variety and change. Easily bored with single-minded thinking. Creative. Likes variety and constantly looking for other options and ventures. Keeps life exciting. Has boundaries but is reasonable and open to negotiation. Relies on self discipline to stay within the structure. An outgoing people loving person. Positive with a sense of humor. A leader and team player.

Chocolate Chip Cookie Dough Ice Cream

Unique and creative. Finds the magic in simple things. Full of surprises and keeps life interesting. This scoop of greatness doesn't need to wave a red flag to attract attention. After you pass the first chilly inspection, (they will look you over before opening to show you more) lots of riches are in store.. A team player, moldable and willing to change, easily bored without variety and creativity. Not a logical detailed person. Doesn't follow a set pattern.

Chocolate Ice Cream Fudge Ball with Caramel Sauce and Nuts

Round, self contained, a whole. Rich, smooth, unique and rewarding. Unlimited in creative use of extremes, from the warm free flowing sweet caramel sauce to the chilly tartness of chocolate and don't forget the crunchy nuggets of wisdom.. Loves spontaneity. Open to change and new experiences. A real feeler. Like to experience life.. Adventuresome.

Coffee Ice Cream with Caramel Sauce and Nuts

Creative and daringly different. A team player, spontaneous and flexible. Likes variety and uniqueness. Moldable and willing to change position. A detail person. An excellent communicator. Very specific and speaks with clarity. Nutty and fun, free flowing and changeable, and makes a lasting impression. Dares to experiment with new ideas.

Homemade Peppermint Ice Cream

Goes the extra mile to make life special. A real pleaser. Full of crunchy treasures. Makes life fun and rewarding. A stimulator. Adds a special spice to life that opens others to their true potential. A natural teacher. Moldable, takes many forms. Makes the best of whatever comes. Creative. Drops hints, a tease. Soft boundaries but can put on the big chill when one gets too close. May appear plain on the outside. Take a deeper look...this one is full of surprises.

Homemade Peppermint Ice Cream Recipe

4 to 6 eggs well beaten	$\frac{1}{2}$ gallon milk
1 large can evaporated milk	1 cup crushed peppermint candies
1 quart half and half milk	$\frac{1}{3}$ cup white Karo syrup
2 cups sugar	Rock Salt
2 tablespoons vanilla	ice for freezer
1 gallon freezer serves 20-24.	

Beat eggs with electric mixer. Add vanilla, Karo syrup, sugar, and mix together. To crush candy, unwrap pieces and place in a plastic sandwich bag and hit with a hammer. Slowly add peppermint to mixture and blend together. Finally, add half and half, and evaporated milk. Pour mixture into a gallon container. Pour in milk to the fill line. Freeze in electric or hand-turned freezer. Use 1 part Rock Salt to 7 parts ice.

Recipe courtesy of Marilyn Neuber Crotty, Albuquerque, New Mexico

Low Fat Yogurt

Unique, creative, ever changing, moldable, swirly, and fun loving. Spontaneous and free flowing. Sensitive to other people's opinions. Demands freedom and space. Likes to be noticed and strives to be a stand-out. A team player...builds off other people and their ideas. Recognizes few limits in life. Knows what they like and will express it.

Strawberry Hot Fudge Sundae

This outwardly fun and playful soul likes to be seen and noticed. A definite pleaser. Alluring and inviting on the outside. A tease. Will first open then close the door. The rich, dark, hot fudge beneath the strawberries and whipped cream topping says "WHOA". Beneath the protective chocolate layer is a sensitive, gentle, smooth, creamy being filled with treasures and surprises. Has a tendency to go from one extreme to another. Likes variety and dares to be different. Spontaneous and free flowing. Structured and layered. Likes rituals and flare.

~ PIE PEOPLE ~

Focused and on target. The planner-goal setter. Tenaciously stays with the plan. Honorable boundaries. Begins with the end in mind people. Knows where they are going. Specific and detailed. Good communicators and decision makers. Thinkers and feelers...right and left brained. Goes for completion. Self-disciplined. Cream pies are compassionate, caring, sensitive and feeling. They balance work and play.

Be specific when communicating with these people. Give them the details and get out of the way. Given the correct tools they can build empires. When the going gets tough, they will detach from any outside influences and be totally dedicated to the results. Concentration and dedication are their strengths.

Easy to work with, they will let you know what they need. Excellent auditory and listening skills make them master communicators.

~ Pie People Affirmation ~

I consistently align with the creamy richness of life, building delicious sweet creations.

Apple Pie

The care taker. Salt of the earth. Everyone's favorite because they are dependable. A true and loyal friend. Keeps things light and fun. A focused, organized, planner but flexible if necessary. An excellent communicator. Doesn't like to argue. It is not important to be right. Gets along with everybody and tends to their business. Content with self. Doesn't need to grab attention. A joyful spirit. The cinnamon flavor is both stimulating and encouraging as well as full of mirth.

Buttermilk Pie

An expressive person, reflective and open. This planner and goal setter usually speaks his mind. A sweet-tart combination. Adventurous. No hidden secrets. What you see is what you get. Consistent with who they are. Leaves a lasting impression.

Cheesecake

Very smooth and easy going. Likes to be liked but doesn't have to be center stage. A loyal friend. Focused and stays on track. A planner who strives to be organized and efficient. A pleasurable experience. Won't try to sell themselves. Believes in self and has definite opinions. Prefers to stay with the familiar. Doesn't like drastic changes. A traditionalist. Consistent...the same from first bite to last. Reflective. Right and left brained thinker-feeler. Likes to barter.

Cheesecake with Strawberries

Single purposed with a plan. A nurturing caring person. Smooth and rewarding. Honorable boundaries and strives to be noticed. The red topping denotes high energy, attracting and stimulating, the playful side. An instigator. Draws people to them. Likes to be attractive and draw attention. Willing to go the extra mile. Will give more than receive. First impulse is to be spontaneous but then tends to be cautious and may override first decision.

Cherry Pie

A fun lover. A sweet-tart stimulator. A bit of a planner but flexible when little cherries roll out of the pie. Rolls along enjoying life. Creative and open to looking for other options. A high energy, people-oriented person. A tease...

Brownie Bottom Pie

Vanilla ice cream caught between a hot fudge topping and a rich fudge brownie. They run from one extreme to another. Sees things as either black or white. The basic nature is focused and contained within tight boundaries, while on the top side they tend to appear spontaneous and free flowing. The vanilla ice cream is moldable but chilly. Wants to look things over before plunging ahead. This part is nurturing and caring, a softy at heart. The hot fudge topping is a camouflage to protect those sensitive feelings. A team player. The anchor man. Adventuresome and fun.

Chocolate Meringue Pie

Fun side up! The light fluffy meringue tells of an outer facade of a carefree and easy style. Doesn't appear to take life too seriously. However, beneath the fluffy exterior there is a serious side. Single focused, they like to complete one task before starting another. Has the ability to concentrate and stay with a project. A loyal friend who likes to have his way, but willing to change his position to avoid conflict. Sees thing as black or white. Goes from one extreme to the other. Vacillates. Pits duty against desire.

Coconut Meringue Pie

Fun loving. Enjoys life. Full of special treasures and rewards. Sensitive, caring and goal oriented. Completes each project before tackling another. Appearance and neatness is important. A perfectionist with a regal appearance. Tempts and lures.

Custard Pie

Consistent and satisfied. Stays with the basics. Content to remain the same. Able to find pleasure in the moment. Not especially outgoing or assertive. Steady and reliable. Keeps life simple. Focused and on track. Add nutmeg for excitement. Handles repetition well.

Death by Chocolate

This rich, chocolate covered Rocky Road ice cream on a crumbled chocolate cookie crust dares and deifies. Beneath the two dark protective outer layers lies a soft creamy goodness filled with delightful surprises. Not visible at first glance is the fun loving softy inside. Serious and structured. Dedicated to a cause and tenaciously focused. Self contained and disciplined. However, look closely and you will find a real feeling, sensitive person on the inside. The longer you know them, the more surprises they reveal. Don't let the protective shield fool you. This person can play.

French Silk Pie

Distinguished with poise and direction. Dares to be different and unique. Serious about commitments and duty. Focused and dedicated. A planner with goals. This serious nature is hidden under a reflective magnet of creamy topping that shows a consistency of character. Structured, proper, consistent, and somewhat opinionated. Sees black and white. Rich...take in small portions. Savor the experience. Leaves a definite impression. Addictive.

Key Lime Pie

Tart, sweet and direct. On task with high energy. An action person who speaks up for what they want. An expert or specialist in one area. Consistent. Logical and fact oriented. "Just the facts, please." Likes things done NOW. Beneath the tartness is a real compassionate nature.

Lemon Chiffon Pie with Raspberry Topping

High energy person who attracts others. Spontaneous on topside but focused with a plan. Always open to a good detour as long as it will accomplish the primary goal. A creative fun lover always in the action. Will defend self with a quick retort when threatened. A stand out in a crowd. A motivator. Honest and says what he thinks. Takes a stand. Stimulates and encourages.

Lemon Meringue Pie

Appears carefree, spontaneous, light and fun, but capable of a quick retort when threatened or intimidated. Can stimulate with fiery rebuffs. Likes challenging conversations. Will spice up any crowd. Focused and single minded but soft boundaries. Open and vulnerable. Easy to know and fun to be with. An excellent teacher.

Pecan Pie

The focused planner. Organized at handling and arranging details. A thinker who puts out an enticing invitation of the richness to come but then is somewhat defensive. Wants to look people over. Self-protective and only close friends get through the exterior nutty portion to know the sensitive person below. Intense and serious but with a sense of humor. Dedicated to a cause.

Pumpkin Chiffon Pie

A smooth rich creamy exterior with a spicy treat hidden inside. Soft flexible boundaries. Consistent and smooth. The kind of person you never tire of. Soft, fluffy and non-intimidating. The soft crumbly crust is further evidence of a dislike for conflict and argument. The white whipped topping is inviting.

Strawberry, Kiwi, Mandarin Orange topped Cream Cheese Pie

Organized, efficient, color coordinated and focused. This outer attracts you to the inner creamy rich nurturing goodness below. An unusual combination. Rich and rewarding. Goal setter but handles several options at once. A leader with grace and style. An achiever who dares to be different. Creative and high energy. Needs variety. Willing to try new combinations but will study them closely first. Very thorough.

Strawberry Pie

A magnet for attracting people. Likes to be noticed. Lots of energy. Stimulates and motivates others. Seed planter. Focused in one specific area. Starts out orderly and arranged but usually will change position.. Needs a crust or support structure to stay within set guidelines. Lots of energy...never seems to run out.

Triple Layer Ice Cream Pie with Fudge Sauce

Creative thinker. Competitive. Likes to be different...unique. Captivating. A perfectionist with rigid boundaries. A high achiever who goes the extra mile. Puts on a good show but has a secret side. Stays frozen to all but a few close friends who know the real person. Likes variety and challenges. A mental planner with attention to details. A high set of standards. Very structured and focused. Stays on target.

~ PUDDING PEOPLE ~

Care-free and spontaneous. Takes any shape or form. Go with the flow/be here now people. Doesn't like too much structure. Don't fence me in. Extremely creative, expressive, feeling, sensitive and compassionate. Has soft boundaries and is easily influenced by others. This openness is a gift when coupled with self discernment. Extremely coachable and fast learners when they are about their bliss. They do not have the self-discipline to override their own bliss for very long. It is difficult for them to be dedicated to something that doesn't bring them joy. When about their business, life flows.

They don't like to make decisions or commit too far in advance since they may want to change their minds. They prefer to go without plans. They gracefully ride the tides of life. Care takers and peace makers.

Use clarity when speaking with pudding people. Ask for a commitment. Limit the decisions making to two choices if you are in a hurry. As reflectors and people pleasers, they create an inner civil war of duty over desire. "What I want to do vs what I think would make you happy thinking" makes decision making strenuous. They are easy going and fun is a must.

Pudding People learn best by hands-on-experience. Details and instructions are conforming and limiting to them. Creative and eager, they often jump to conclusions without all the facts. It is okay however, as they are so open and life continues to send them the messages. They seem to always get it at just the right time. They flow through life with the greatest of ease.

Pudding People Affirmation

I easily flow with Divine confection, blending and folding for sweet rewards.

Banana Pudding

A likable easy going person full of fun surprises. Content with self. Doesn't need to sell self. Caring and sympathetic. Spontaneous. Doesn't like to make plans and set goals. Likes to let life happen. Likes variety and gets bored with long range projects. Everyone's favorite. Smooth and rewarding. Full of exciting hidden treats. Sensitive.

Bread Pudding

Warm and inviting, this person is everyone's favorite. Unpretentious, a likable personality and easy to know but has a sensitive nature. Mushy when it comes to taking a stand. Avoids conflict. Moderate boundaries and sympathetic to causes. Content with life and satisfied with life style. Not especially competitive. Keeps life simple and able to be creative with basics. Full of hidden surprises. Don't let the plainness of the outer packaging fool you. Tends to be spontaneous but then on second thought reverts to caution.

Chocolate Pudding, Mousse or Soufflé

Single-purposed. Focuses on one thing at a time and likes to finish it before starting another project. Content with self. Doesn't need to seek recognition and approval of others. Has a lot of substance. Earthy. Spontaneous and moldable with soft boundaries. A serious side but not pushy. Goes with the flow. A peace maker. A smooth and rewarding experience. Mousse has a lighter side. Keeps inner feelings and deepest thoughts for intimate friends..

Chocolate Souffl, Recipe

4 T. butter	5 T. flour
1/4 t. salt	1 c. milk
2 oz. Baker's chocolate	3 eggs
1/2 t. vanilla	1/2 c. sugar

Melt the butter; add the flour and cook until bubbly. Add milk, salt and melted chocolate. Stir constantly until thick. Cool. Beat egg yolks. Add vanilla and continue beating until smooth and creamy. Fold into the egg yolks the stiffly beaten egg whites, to which sugar has been added as in a meringue. Fold egg mixture into chocolate sauce. Pour into a baking dish and set in a pan of hot water. Bake 1 hour at 350 degrees. Serve with a raspberry glaze.

Creme Bruelee or Flan

Rich, creamy, moldable...fits any shape. Spontaneous. Doesn't like to be boxed in, moves in circles rather than straight lines. Stays with one game plan. Dares to be different in a sophisticated sort of way. Chic. Soft boundaries. Will change direction. Not adamant about having own way. Sweetly enticing.

Honey

Sweet and charming. Naive and unpretentious. Content with self. An open book to all. Not a deceiver. Honesty and integrity are strong values. Dependable and reliable. Doesn't like to make decisions or take the lead. Spontaneous and free flowing. Easy going and gets along with everyone. Sweet but can sting when cornered.

Jell-O

Lots of clarity and purpose. Honesty and integrity are important values. Very likable and agreeable. Has a definite shape but will fit any mold. Open to change and finding the best solutions. Doesn't mind changing position. Has lots of variety and options. Versatile. A favorite with everyone. Not a scene stealer. Content with self. Loose and flexible. Emotional and feeling. Sensuous.

Lemon Chiffon Souffl, with Raspberry Sauce

Light, fluffy and full of fun. Tart-sweet. Can and will fire zingers when necessary. Dry wit and delightful sense of humor. Will make a point with humor. Moldable. Loves to experience extremes. Adventuresome. Reflective and analytical. A stimulator. Wants to be noticed and accepted. Gives something extra. An encourager and supporter. Very people oriented. A team player. Willing to try something new just for the fun of it.

Strawberries Romanoff

Regal and elegant. Creative and different. Layered and efficient. Rich, creamy, smooth with hidden surprises. Nurturing and compassionate. A team player who takes any shape. Agreeable and easy to work with. Reflective. A mind stimulator.

Strawberries Romanoff

1 pint Vanilla Ice Cream   3 T. Cointreau
1 c. whipped cream   ½ c. confectioners' sugar
6 T. Cointreau   6 chilled stemmed glasses
1 quart fresh slightly mashed
strawberries

Whip vanilla ice cream until creamy and fold in whipped cream, then add 6 tablespoons of Cointreau. Fold in strawberries, sweetened with confectioners' sugar and 3 tablespoons of Cointreau. Blend quickly and lightly. Serve in chilled, stemmed glass.

Tapioca Pudding

Fits any mold. Free flowing and spontaneous. A peacemaker. Gives a little extra. Compassionate and caring. Sympathetic to a cause. Consistent with who and what they are. Creative without boundaries or limitations. Avoids too much structure and rigid rules.

Smooth and creamy. Light and enjoyable. Stays with what works. A team player...goes with many things. Everybody's favorite. Sensuous and fun. The type you can't get enough of.

Vanilla Pudding

Free flowing and spontaneous. A peacemaker. Consistent with who and what they are. Content and satisfied. Creative without boundaries or limitations. Avoids too much structure and rigid rules. Smooth and creamy. A caretaker. Light and enjoyable. Stays with what works. Reflective...a natural teacher. Doesn't like to make decisions.

Whipped Cream

Takes any shape or form and has fun doing it. Will swirl, peak, blop or fold. Adds zest to life. A real team player. Goes with anything. A smooth enriching experience. Sees the good in others and tells them about it. Reflective. Open and consistent. Doesn't withhold from others. A real giver. Spontaneous and changeable within one basic plan. An expert in one primary area. A softy at heart and smooth with words.

White Chocolate Mousse

Light and fluffy. Keeps things simple. Reflective, teaches by example. Open and honest. Integrity is a strong value. Doesn't hold back or hide thoughts. Expresses feelings easily. Moldable and open to change. Good listening skills. Flexible boundaries. Content and consistent with who they are.

~ Unique or Combination People ~

Dare to be different. Adventuresome. Creative. Team players. Unlimited. Action people. Will go the extra mile. Achievers.

This high energy group gets things done. Don't bore them with trivia.. Give them the big picture and the space to create it. Don't limit them with too much structure and limiting procedure.

Creative innovators, they will push the envelope on new and exciting ideas. Risk takers and pioneers, they venture into the unknown and love challenges. Inspiring and contagious.

These unique personalities overlap into the other categories. Look for structure clues for more specific details.

~ Unique or Combination People Affirmation ~

Smooth combinations of originality, organization, structure and purpose pour through me achieving rich, rewarding results.

Anything Chocolate

Does not like limitations. "Don't fence me in!!" Freedom and space to create are strong values. Focuses on a primary subject but allows variations within a specific area regarding that subject. Specific communicator. Straight forward. Organized and intense when working. Takes action and stays on task. Likes completion and results. Doesn't like to drag things out. Avoids intimacy accept with close friends. Avoids getting too personal with strangers. A team player who likes variety and options. A leader.

Baked Alaska

Unique and elegant. Sophisticated and grand in appearance. Very structured, organized, focused and determined. A rewarding experience to those that know them. Full of richness and treasures. True giver. Loves to entertain. A team manager who pulls things together.. Has a high set of values. Talented in a variety of different things and uses them well. Likes to be different.

Baked Alaska Recipe

1 box yellow or white cake mix
ice cream (one or more flavors)
2 oz. brandy
black cherries or freshly sugared strawberries

4 egg whites stiffly beaten
$3/4$ c. powdered sugar
corn starch

Place a layer of any white or yellow cake on an oven-proof dish. If you are fond of rum or brandy, sprinkle the cake generously with either or both, and a fine layer of granulated sugar. Cover with a thick layer of vanilla ice cream, softened, then add another flavor of your choice. Leave a half-inch "frame around the cake. Freeze until the ice cream is firm. Then pile high and cover completely with meringue made from beating the egg whites until stiff and then adding the powdered sugar. Brown quickly in a 450 degree oven, then remove. Add black cherries slightly thickened with cornstarch or fresh sugared strawberries around the tray. Pour 1 ounce of brandy on the tray, light and serve at once. This is for 1 quart of ice cream.

Cannoli

Humorous and light. Doesn't appear to take life to seriously. Has honorable boundaries on the outside but a real pushover to those who are close. Self disciplined and regimented and runs within their space. Full of rich creamy goodness and hidden surprises. Don't let the outer flakiness fool you. There is a real caring, nurturing person inside. Really worth getting to know.

Chocolate After Dinner Mint

Refreshing. Uplifting, smooth and nurturing. Rich. Take in small amounts to savor the flavor. Dynamite comes in a small package. Don't over look the power in this delicate morsel. Make lasting impressions. A flavor that last. You will want more. Don't rush the experience. There is a surprise beneath the dark chocolate protective outer coating. Some are round and soft in the middle, some oblong and solid. It makes a difference. Ask for clarification.

Chocolate Eclair

Unique, creative and full of surprises. The rich chocolate coating alerts you to the goodness inside. The crusty shell tells of strong boundaries. It's airy texture shows an openness to learning and trying new ideas. The contradicting values of the spontaneous flow of the chocolate and the hard protective shell creates an inner civil war. Within lies the true jewel...creamy, smooth, consistent, and nurturing. Dignified, it stands alone.

Cotton Candy

Light, fluffy, flexible. Extremely changeable. Sweet and enticing. Enfolds and sticks. A people pleasers. Pleasant to the eye and palate. Everybody's favorite. Fun! Playful. The changeable style that makes them who and what they are. Spiraling outward. Always seeking another perspective. A specialist in one field. Stands alone.

Cream Puff

Aspiring and unique. The crusty shell is a protective boundary. Stands alone. Self contained. A specialist in one area. Likes moments of solitude. An internal thinker and cautious observer. Doesn't like to be rushed or forced to make decisions. The powdered sugar topping gently hints at the rich reward inside. Content with who and what they are. You must gain their trust slowly. A natural reflective teacher. Strong spiritual foundation. Stays with what's comfortable.

English Trifle

Full of surprises. Versatile and exciting. Adventuresome. A creator and builder. Resourceful. Demands variety...easily bored without it. Sensitive and compassionate, caring and giving. Elegant and unique. A real softy. A natural teacher with an inquisitive nature. Moldable, open to new ideas and challenges change. Nothing boring here. Tighten your skates because they are always up to something new. A high energy stimulator. Can handle multiple projects at once. Makes lasting friends. Holds things together. The Matriarch of the family.

Here is a bonus from The Jensky Family Cookbook, "Sharing Recipes" by Madelyn Miller. Estelle Plous cooked fabulous meals everyday when Madelyn was growing up. Even after Madelyn became a Restaurant Reviewer, her favorite place to eat was still her mom's house. Try this recipe and you will know why.

English Trifle Recipe

2 frozen pound cakes, cut into ½ inch pieces (Sara Lee preferred)

2 jiggers Apricot or Peach Brandy or Cointreau

2 ½ quarts fresh strawberries, washed and sliced (reserve a few whole ones
   with stems for garnish.

6 bananas, sliced

2 (1 lb.) cans vanilla pudding (Thank You brand preferred)

1 (18 oz.) jar apricot preserves

1 (20 oz.) carton whipped topping, thawed

Cut away the cake's crust and line bottom of a large, deep glass dessert dish or trifle bowl with the cake slices. Sprinkle cake with apricot brandy or Cointreau if desired. Spread half the apricot preserves over the cake, then add half the sliced bananas and strawberries, placing them carefully over the cake. Spread half the whipped topping over the fruit.

Now repeat each of the layers, except use the pudding rather than the whipped topping. Finish with a layer of cake topped with the remaining preserves and the rest of the whipped topping . Decorate with whole strawberries with the stems still on and chill at least 4 hours or overnight. Serve in chilled dessert dishes.

For an excellent variation use raspberries or flavored preserves.

English Truffle

Highly concentrated and can stand alone. A little goes along way. Rich beyond measure. An observatory shape. Ever searching, scanning. Controls emotions and feelings. Keeps personal life private. Unrevealing. Self disciplined and dedicated. Once you penetrate the outer chocolate coating succulent surprises await the patient victor.

Fudge

Rich, smooth, creamy. A flavor that lasts. This high achiever comes with self imposed perimeters. Self disciplined, they stay on task and are tenacious about finishing a project. Concentration and focus are strong qualities. They prefer working alone and often withdraw to quite places. Self driven, they rarely disclose their inner secrets. Delicious but take in small amounts.

Marshmallow

Light and reflective, a natural teacher. Tender with soft boundaries...sensitive but doesn't hold grudges. Tends to keep life light and humorous. Positive. Always looks for another option. Open to hearing the other side. Centered around a core belief system. Spiritual. Makes lasting friendships. Loyal.

Napoleon

Elegant with a definite touch of class. Rich and rewarding. Structured...a builder. Uses resources in unique combinations to create a rich reward. A team player but demands order. Self defined boundaries but can change if the majority demands it. Teachers by example rather than lecturing. Flaky layers of pastry keep life light yet combine to form a tough protective layer. Not a push over, even though they look sweet and delicate. The sweet icing on top lets you know of the TLC inside. An earth angel.

Sugar Glazed Donut

Sweet and inviting. A real treat. A circle within a circle. Stays within self defined boundaries. An expert in a specialized area. Soft, spongy, open to learning. An inquisitive thinker. Always searching for other options and creative ideas. Makes life fun. Keeps life light and simple. A finger-lickin' experience. Addictive. A reflective teacher.

QUESTIONABLE PEOPLE

~ DESSERT DILEMMAS! ~

Can't Decide or Baffled

An unlimited being who is a free spirit and cannot see themselves contained in any one dessert. This creative unique person thrives on variety and embraces change and challenges. Will not limit their spontaneity by fencing themselves into a restricted environment. Flexible and free flowing. Is truly baffled by the question. Lighthearted and good natured.

Refuses to Play

A perfectionist with self proclaimed rules and boundaries. Likes to lead and set procedure. Avoids self disclosure. Self protecting and opinionated. A cautious analyzer who likes to think things through thoroughly without pressure. Wants to taste the icing before taking a big slice. A real thinker. Takes a stand and sticks to it. Likes facts and results. Non-emotional. Prioritizes.

PART THREE:

Claiming
Your Sweet Rewards!

❀ Creating It in Your Life

❀ An Extra Serving

❀ Full and Content

❀ The Icing on the Cake

~ CREATING IT IN YOUR LIFE ~

You have just finished the last bite of the dessert analogies and are now ready to create some FUN on your own. Remember when we accept and understand people for the Sweet Rewards and Delicious Desserts they are, we will receive our own Sweet Rewards.

Ask of friends, family members and co-workers, "What can we create together?" Let your life be a reflection of the tasty morsels which can only be found when two or more desserts create together.

Look for ways to whip up something delightful. The structured and focused chocolate layer cake will get a variety of ideas from the fun loving, spontaneous and creative strawberry shortcake. Together they are much more than any individual dessert. And just think how boring life would be if we were all the same dessert.

Go out into the world and CREATE something new and different in your life. Dare to have FUN and to fully participate in your very own Celebration of Life! Embrace not only all of the similarities you notice in others, but all of the unique differences others contribute to our world of Just Desserts.

Someone once said the definition of a friend is a person who agrees with you, and has the same likes and dislikes as you. Break out of this mind set and allow yourself to experience a different kind of friend. You may find the key to embracing others is in embracing all of your own unique ingredients fully.

Enjoy Your Own Sweet Rewards!

~ An Extra Serving ~

This section of the book is something extra. It is being included for two very different reasons. First, and as mentioned earlier, for those who are resisting making a commitment to kick the training wheels off and to fully experience their ride through life. This section is my gift to you! I feel by completing the "Commitment Process" worksheet towards a goal you wish to accomplish, you will choose to go for all that life is offering each of us.

In addition to this process and the worksheet, I have included the Personality Profile Worksheet used in "People Are Just Desserts Seminars", which is designed primarily for couples and for those considering.... This worksheet is designed to be a starting point from which we compare similarities and differences with those of our partner in a non-judgmental and accepting fashion.

The Personality Worksheet and the scoring sheets have been included to give you an idea of the areas of our life which we will touch on during the two and a half day seminar. It will also give you and your partner an opportunity to notice your similarities and to experience what it feels like to fully embrace your differences. How's that for S-T-R-E-T-C-H-I-N-G! Go ahead, give life a GO and have FUN in living it!

The "Commitment Process"

CAUTION: *This process WORKS! It should only be used when you are ready for a change in your life! Go ahead, get Committed and Choose to create your own Celebration of Life!...*

This is a tool that will greatly assist you in moving purposefully towards your goals in life. It will take conscious effort and practice. It will work if you choose to allow it to become a part of your life. If you have a desire to get more of what you want out of life, and to identify what is important, you will have success using this tool. Go ahead, dare to create your own Celebration of Life!

The Courage to Choose What you Want in Life
(or Commitment in One Easy Lesson!)

When choosing what you want to create in your life, you may notice a resistance to choosing with full intention - that is, with *commitment*. You may find yourself feeling anxious, worrying about the future, or automatically choosing to work on an area which is fairly trivial and easy to change. If you are feeling this way, consider looking at commitment a different way.

Most people think commitment is an obligation or an inflexible or unbreakable promise. When looking at commitment from this perspective, you will find yourself worrying about the future, demanding guarantees and becoming obsessed with fears about things which may not turn out exactly as you want them. You may even feel trapped. When you operate *from the belief* that commitment robs you of your free will or choice, you will not take action. In the end, you either give up what you want, or, worse yet, resent the very thing you wanted most.

Commitment is the courage to make a choice!

Commitment is choice. It is the energy of action as opposed to that of inaction. It is the expression of freedom and spontaneity, not the opposite of it. How can you express your freedom except through choice, in deciding what to go for in life?

Commitment then requires a unique and difficult kind of acceptance - a faith in the future - a willingness to accept what will be and, therefore, living in the present. This is why it requires courage!

The opposite of commitment is inaction - not choosing at all - which is based on a lack of faith. It is an unhealthy attachment to the future - a fear of the unknown, a need for guarantees, a need to know there will be no regrets, or a need for acceptance or approval. Inaction is based on fear of failure, the opposite of spontaneity.

A misunderstanding of commitment is the main reason why people who can't or won't face limits (many people in prison), have the least spontaneity and freedom in their lives. They refuse to conform to rules and structure. They see it as loosing freedom. They constantly justify doing life "their way." They tend to have addictions (addictions are a clear example of losing the ability to choose - drugs, food, relationships, sex, abuse, etc.) and tend to live *reactively* instead of *proactively*.

When your goal in living becomes having no limits, you lose the ability to act because you demand things turn out as you want. You set yourself up for disappointment after disappointment after disappointment. The more you *demand* your freedom and spontaneity, the less freedom and spontaneity you will have in your life because you will be afraid to be free and spontaneous, to choose.

Fear of losing something almost always creates the loss which we most fear.

This loss occurs because the person possessed by the need for freedom, is afraid of the limits which their own choices create. They would rather suffer from what they perceive as random circumstances (what life hands us on a daily basis) than the "limits" of expressing their own freedom. It is an illusion with a very high price. Unfortunately, few people get the lesson because of their tendency to protect their illusion of freedom with rationalizations. Instead of recognizing they are not free because they are afraid to choose, they use other people or the events they draw into their lives to explain their loss of freedom. They consistently feel "trapped". They consistently withdraw from life, because they are trying so desperately to be free. The more they struggle the more confined they feel. They way out is to have purpose, to commit, to consciously choose and live that choice fully until it is no longer serving you or others.

Commitment and living in the moment may seem paradoxical. How can you commit yourself to something, plan for the future, and let the future go at the same time? Commitment is not deciding how the future will be, which is of course impossible. You cannot do it no matter what because this is fully in the grips of the Mystery~, not any individual. Hold the thought that anything can happen in your life! Commitment is going for something now, in this moment, and the next, and then the next. It is living. It is conscious self-expression of what you want to achieve. It is a personal Celebration of Life!

A good analogy is to think of a river. A river flows to the ocean. It does not worry it might hit a rock or be evaporated. It accepts what is, but does not resist, give up, runaway, or resent gravitational pull, rocks or mountains. When it hits an obstacle it looks for the easiest way to fulfill its intention - another way. If it is evaporated it does not have regrets that it did not get to the ocean, but instead expresses itself in a new equally valuable way.

To make an even small commitment, one must do several things:

1. Consciously choose one thing you want to create in your life. To do this, explore your deeper purposes. Examine your intentions.
2. Look at your motivation in creating this in your life.
3. Be willing to fail.
4. Be willing to accept both the pleasure and the pain in creating it in your life.
5. Lighten up!

Perhaps more should be said about #4. Why should you be willing to do anything that might bring you pain? The reason we have pain is because the human ego is not always cooperative. It makes judgments about your experiences and in doing so misinterprets, distorts and creates suffering. Up to now I have talked about the ideal. In reality, I am rarely able to attain this kind of unconditional acceptance for all I create in my life, including pain. From time to time I create suffering due to my resistance.

Although I know I am being unreasonable about the demands I place on myself, I make matters worse by worrying about my unreasonableness. In other words, I suffer because of my suffering. Now I have decided that at times I will suffer... So what! I can't die, nor can I live trying to minimize suffering by trying to control everything. So, I have decided I will simply have any sufferings I choose to have. It just is. Which brings us to #5, lightening up. Remember, angels can fly because they take themselves *lightly*.

When I get tired of the pain, I ask my higher source, "How can I see this differently?" When I cannot change the event or situation, like as not, the only thing I can change is my perception. When I sold my home of some twenty years I created a painful situation. I beat myself up over the fact I could not pre-determine the values of the family that bought it. Their needs and values for the home were different than mine. In short they were not caring for the property the way I had. I felt guilty and responsible to this house that had given so much love and protection to my family. I decided to change my perception. I chose to believe the house selected this family as they really needed love and it had lots of love to give. It made the letting go much easier. The house was fulfilling a deeper purpose. I shifted my perception and with it my pain.

The Commitment Process is about getting committed. Pick an important goal in your life. Look at your intention in creating this in your life and create this dream while using this new definition of commitment. Notice any resistance, and try to identify the underlying fear.

If you experience resistance ask yourself...

1. Am I afraid of the unknown?
2. Am I demanding guarantees?
3. Am I demanding no regrets?
4. Am I afraid of losing spontaneity?
5. Am I afraid of failure or ridicule?
6. Am I afraid of responsibility that comes with attaining this goal?
7. Am I satisfied with my purpose?

Next, try for a moment, letting go of your fears. Tell yourself you want this. You are committed to attaining this, and at each moment you will have the freedom to choose going for it or not. Notice how it feels to have faith in your ability to deal with whatever comes - the ability to face the unknown.

Now, decide how you will begin to attain this - at each step recognizing you are choosing this action as an expression of what you have chosen. Write out your actions as specifically as possible. The more specifically you imagine your actions, the more likely it is you will follow through with them. Be sure to date, and commit to each action on a specific day and even a time of day if possible.

Continue with the Commitment Process by doing your visualization. Imagine yourself vividly performing each action. Notice how it feels. Do you feel as if you "want to" or "have to" perform these actions? If you "have to", go back and look at fears again, or look at your intention (purpose). More than likely, you will find performing these imaginary actions pleasurable and satisfying.

Finally, look at possible methods of support. Find at least two people who want you to make it in life, who have as one of their goals your happiness in life. Be sure and clearly define what support looks like and is most effective for you. Don't hold back.

Remember, you want this!

~ The "Commitment Process" ~

MY COMMITMENT - (What I want to create in my life): State a desired "want" or a goal on life in a present tense form as though it already exists:

MY MOTIVATION - (Why I want to create this in my life): Bring to your mind and heart every reason, or "motivator", you can and then create a statement of motivation to further your goal.

VISUALIZE - Imagine or picture yourself already having created the intended goal. Notice how it feels and notice if you would like to refine your "Commitment" in any fashion.

MY ACTIONS - (I Choose to take these actions): Make a series of specific steps or agreements with yourself (And at least one other support partner) about what you choose to do to create the desired goal in your life. Be specific and date your actions:

1) _____ Date:_____

2) _____ Date:_____

3) _____ Date:_____

4) _____ Date:_____

5) _____ Date _____

VISUALIZE - Imagine or picture yourself actually completing the "Action" steps as listed above. Take each one slowly and notice in full sensory proportion every step of every action which will create your results. Notice what you are feeling as you complete each action. Notice any "Self Talk" that may creep into your picture which you can clear. Actually create these action steps several times a day, visually, then implement them in the physical on schedule as shown above. You may refine your action steps as is necessary to further you in creating your results.

SUPPORT - Ask for support from at least one other person to assist you on a daily basis in reviewing your actions, agreements and intentions. This person's support and interest will help you in staying on purpose and creating any intended result you desire in your life. Clearly define what this support role will look like:

ADDITIONAL NOTES: List any notes you may find helpful in creating this "want" or goal in your life. Consider also listing any persistent self-talk which is finding its way into the process. Giving it a place of its own will allow it to be cleared from your mind and in turn open a clear path for your creation to unfold.

Savor the Sweet Rewards of Commitment!

"People Are Just Desserts"

Personal Profile Worksheet

Directions: Circle the number on the scale from 0 to 6 after each statement. The number will indicate how often or how well the statement applies to you. Answer the questions in terms of the past six months. Feel free to add any notes you may choose in the comments column. (No notes are necessary and as an example you may write: "This is a recent change", or "This is probably due to work stress", etc.)

Never		Sometimes			Always	
0	1	2	3	4	5	6

#	Statement	Rating	Comments
1	It's OK for me to play and be blissfully happy in life.	0 1 2 3 4 5 6	
2	I easily forgive others who have emotionally hurt me in the past.	0 1 2 3 4 5 6	
3	I can effectively recreate my experience in another through verbal communication.	0 1 2 3 4 5 6	
4	I tell my partner about changes in my sexual needs and desires.	0 1 2 3 4 5 6	
5	I am a spiritual being.	0 1 2 3 4 5 6	
6	I participate in some form of cardiovascular exercise at least three times a week for a period of at least 30 minutes.	0 1 2 3 4 5 6	
7	I am financially independent.	0 1 2 3 4 5 6	
8	I know what I want to create in my future.	0 1 2 3 4 5 6	
9	I have fully forgiven myself for all the wrong I have done in my life.	0 1 2 3 4 5 6	
10	I help create a romantic setting for our love-making.	0 1 2 3 4 5 6	
11	I have personally experienced "God" in my life.	0 1 2 3 4 5 6	
12	I attend at several different denominations of religious worship each year.	0 1 2 3 4 5 6	

13	When I tell my partner "I love you", they feel it.	0 1 2 3 4 5 6	
14	I create my own reality.	0 1 2 3 4 5 6	
15	I feel comfortable with the amount of money coming into and going out of my life.	0 1 2 3 4 5 6	
16	I am satisfied with my body weight.	0 1 2 3 4 5 6	
17	I have a high level of self esteem and am proud of my accomplishments in life.	0 1 2 3 4 5 6	
18	I am making a positive difference in the world.	0 1 2 3 4 5 6	
19	I have experienced moments of Heaven on Earth.	0 1 2 3 4 5 6	
20	I rarely notice what race someone is when I am walking in a shopping mall or in a park.	0 1 2 3 4 5 6	
21	I am aware of my posture when meeting someone for the first time.	0 1 2 3 4 5 6	
22	I see happiness, love and contentment in my future.	0 1 2 3 4 5 6	
23	I believe there is a connection between body, mind and spirit.	0 1 2 3 4 5 6	
24	I feel comfortable having my partner see me in the nude.	0 1 2 3 4 5 6	
25	I live below my financial means, not at or above.	0 1 2 3 4 5 6	
26	I am confident of my abilities in being a good parent.	0 1 2 3 4 5 6	
27	I feel that everyone that comes into my life can be my teacher.	0 1 2 3 4 5 6	
28	I have a purpose in life.	0 1 2 3 4 5 6	
29	I appreciate abilities and traits in others which I have not yet discovered in myself.	0 1 2 3 4 5 6	
30	I monitor my cholesterol level and it is below 200.	0 1 2 3 4 5 6	

31	I am aware of my level of energy and drive in life.	0 1 2 3 4 5 6	
32	I have a comfortable way of letting my partner know when I would like to make love.	0 1 2 3 4 5 6	
33	I honor myself and all that I am.	0 1 2 3 4 5 6	
34	I am aware of my net worth as of today.	0 1 2 3 4 5 6	
35	I recognize when I have conflicting purposes in life.	0 1 2 3 4 5 6	
36	When my partner tells me they want to talk to me I give them my full attention regardless of what I am doing.	0 1 2 3 4 5 6	
37	I am environmentally conscious and respect the balance of our ecosystem.	0 1 2 3 4 5 6	
38	I feel that at the core of every person is a common goodness that runs through	0 1 2 3 4 5 6	
39	I can walk 3 miles in 45 minutes and not experience difficulty breathing.	0 1 2 3 4 5 6	
40	I am a growing, changing and evolving person.	0 1 2 3 4 5 6	
41	I live a frugal lifestyle.	0 1 2 3 4 5 6	
42	I view the world as a safe and happy place.	0 1 2 3 4 5 6	
43	I have the ability to change any aspect of my life I so choose.	0 1 2 3 4 5 6	
44	I feel comfortable disclosing personal information about my self when I communicate.	0 1 2 3 4 5 6	
45	I make an effort to learn about significant changes in my partner's sexual needs and desires.	0 1 2 3 4 5 6	
46	I quiet and still myself on a daily basis or participate in a regular daily spiritual practice of some sort.	0 1 2 3 4 5 6	
47	I feel every human being has a larger purpose in life than what is apparent on a surface level.	0 1 2 3 4 5 6	

48	I forgive others easily.	0 1 2 3 4 5 6	
49	I am aware of, and monitor, the amount of fat in my diet.	0 1 2 3 4 5 6	
50	I handle all of my own investments and financial matters personally.	0 1 2 3 4 5 6	
51	I feel I am in harmony with the rest of my world.	0 1 2 3 4 5 6	
52	I can create in reality anything I can dream.	0 1 2 3 4 5 6	
53	I feel there is a spiritual connection between all beings.	0 1 2 3 4 5 6	
54	I experience a spiritual connection with my partner during lovemaking.	0 1 2 3 4 5 6	
55	I feel that through my own abilities and talents I can accomplish anything in life I choose.	0 1 2 3 4 5 6	
56	I maintain an open line of communication with my partner.	0 1 2 3 4 5 6	
57	I am content with my standard of living.	0 1 2 3 4 5 6	
58	I have the ability to create my future in any fashion I choose.	0 1 2 3 4 5 6	
59	I am accepting of others who have life-styles quite different than my own.	0 1 2 3 4 5 6	
60	As we make love, I let my partner know which techniques and positions are most pleasurable to me.	0 1 2 3 4 5 6	
61	I am satisfied with my level of physical wellness.	0 1 2 3 4 5 6	
62	I touch my partner in an intimate fashion several times a day.	0 1 2 3 4 5 6	
63	I recognize and celebrate my wins in life.	0 1 2 3 4 5 6	

"People Are Just Desserts"
Personal Profile Scoring Sheet

Directions:

1) Record the numbers that you circled under each of the statements on the Personal Profile Worksheet. The numbers below correspond to the number in front of each statement.
2) Add up the numbers in each section and write in the total for each section.
3) Plot these totals in the corresponding sections on the "People Are Just Desserts"- Profile Graph. Draw a line connecting your scores.

The Sweet Rewards of Accepting Others		The Sweet Rewards of Self Acceptance		Creating Your Dreams	
2		9		8	
12		17		14	
20		26		22	
29		33		31	
38		42		43	
48		51		52	
59		63		58	
Total		Total		Total	
Communication		**Sexuality**		**Physical Wellness**	
3		4		6	
13		10		16	
21		24		23	
36		32		30	
44		45		39	
56		54		49	
62		60		61	
Total		Total		Total	
Making Peace With Money		**Touching– the Mystery**		**Discovering Your Life Purpose**	
7		5		1	
15		11		18	
25		19		28	
34		27		35	
41		37		40	
50		46		47	
57		53		55	
Total		Total		Total	

"People Are Just Desserts"
Profile Graph

Directions:
1) Plot the totals in the corresponding sections from the "People are Just Desserts" - Personal Profile Scoring Sheet.
2) Draw a line connecting your scores.

Score	Accept Others	Accept Self	Creating Dreams	Comm.	Sexual	Physical Wellness	Peace w/ Money	Touching Mystery	Life Purpose
42									
40									
38									
36									
34									
32									
30									
28									
26									
24									
22									
20									
18									
16									
14									
12									
10									
8									
6									
4									
2									
0									

~ Full and Content ~

I hope the feeling you are now experiencing is one of fullness and contentment. The way you feel when you lay your fork down on the table as you taste the last bite of your dessert after a big holiday meal.

By now I am sure you have rounded up a few friends and family members and have given your new skills a test run! If not, do so right this minute. Experience the fun. Remember, we are all unique and different and each of us has special ingredients. When we blend these ingredients in harmony we always create the perfect Dessert!

May we accept every person in their perfect role...

Remember, under the heading of "every person" comes ourselves...

~ Sweet Affirmations ~

1. *I use my whipped wisdom combined with my sweet knowledge to make tasteful and delicious decisions.*
2. *Smooth layers of organization, structure and purpose pour through me with the richness of cream.*
3. *I blend pure ingredients that rise to every occasion for flavorful results.*
4. *My life is creamy, smooth, rich and delicious.*
5. *Fluffy happiness, juicy joy and scrumptious laughter describe my delightful state of being!*

~ THE ICING ON THE CAKE ~

We are all beautifully blended ingredients and have become a delicious dessert, but often times we just can't see it for ourselves. This exercise is designed to help you identify your inherent Sweetness and in doing so to reveal your Sweet Perfections. You will see you really are the Icing on the Cake!

Simply answer each question or respond to the statement, and have *FUN!*

YOU ARE THE ICING ON THE CAKE!

1. How Sweetly do you see yourself? (List several traits or qualities.)

2. How deliciously do you see others? (Mentally visualize a friend and list several traits or qualities.)

3. Notice and note the similarities in #1 and #2...

4. Notice and note the differences in #1 and #2... (Specifically those traits you noticed in others but didn't see in yourself.)

5. Notice how you feel about the traits or qualities you noticed in others but failed to recognize in yourself. Can you savor the flavor of these traits in yourself now?

6. Will you commit to embracing and savoring all your Sweet Perfections each time you recognize them?

7. Will you commit to carrying a note pad and recording your accomplishments and reviewing them daily?

8. Each week will you commit to writing a rich, fun Dessert Affirmation and read it daily to remind you how scrumptious you are?

9.) Will you commit to looking in the mirror at least twice daily and making the heartfelt statement, "I am the Icing on the Cake!"?

10. Record any notes, affirmations, revelations or other Sweet Pieces you discover about yourself for the coming week in this space. And please, use extra sheets as your list grows.

~ A Closing Touch ~

I hope you have enjoyed "People Are Just Desserts". In my effort to make a contribution to our world, I heartily welcome your comments and suggestions about how I may improve this book for future editions. Please let me know what you have found to be of value as well as what may not have glazed your donut.

Up to now the focus has been on other desserts and personalities. Perhaps it is time to tell you a little more about my particular dessert... and if you have not guessed it by now, I am a Cherries Jubilee! Here are some excerpts from a speakers brochure telling you a little more about this Cherries Jubilee.

Perry A~ stimulates people to open to their dreams and to instigate the joys of life. She is a networker extraordinaire, talented writer, gifted speaker, and seminar developer. Perry A~'s ability to draw people out and reflect for them their unlimited potential is a unique gift. She is a positive force in an oftentimes negative world who demonstrates how to look for and receive Universal Gifts in everyday places. She stresses looking for teachers in unlikely places.

Perry A~'s philosophy is that happiness is found through the contributions we make in the lives of others. She is a country/city girl and the mother of two beautiful daughters, Allyson and Ashley.

A Houston native, Perry A~ graduated from Texas Tech University with a Degree in Agriculture. While in college she was the first coed to be awarded the "Aggie of the Year Award"; was Texas Tech Rodeo Queen; an active member and officer of Zeta Tau Alpha Sorority; she served as treasurer and on the Board of Directors of the Rodeo Club; was a member of the Aggie Club, the Block and Bridle Club and served on the staff of the La Ventana.

Perry A~ spent the next twenty-seven years after college in the small farming community of Seymour, Texas raising children, gardening and being "Ms Volunteer" and "super mom". She joyfully dedicated much of her time supporting her daughters in their 4-H and Quarter Horse activities. Both won state honors with their horses.

After a divorce, and a short career as a probation officer, Perry A~ began opening to a new purpose in life. In 1990, taking advice from her heart, she set out on a new path in life. She began public speaking and writing. Gradually her dream began to take form and in short order it has become a life force of its own. In 1992, in furtherance of this dream, she arrived in Austin, Texas. Today she delivers the message that we are whole and complete just as we are. She instills in everyone she meets a spark of life that encourages them to embrace all of their untapped potential and to 'Go for Life'. Her message is cleverly disguised in Dessert analogies and spiced with Cajun Humor.

Perry A~'s style of humor, and her touching message, a la Just Desserts, provides enrichment, education, enlightenment and enjoyment to the lives of thousands. She is a creative innovator whose wide array of programs reflect her ability to add spice to life. She presents an exciting learning forum, offering life lessons in an entertaining format. You will laugh and enjoy as the messages hit home.

So there you have it, Perry A~ in a nutshell! But what you don't yet know is about the rest of my dessert tray... Here is a small sampler!

~ OTHER SWEETS NOW AVAILABLE ~

"Thank You For Listening...
But I Wasn't Quite Through!"

A book of Perry A~'s favorite lifetime personal stories. A moving collection of her experiences living life to the fullest while growing up in Texas.

"A Touch of Daisies"

A book of affirmations... Bright Spots for Sunny Days. These affirmations are the result of a group of earth angels who met weekly in Austin to support one another in creating their dreams using the Master Mind Principle...'Where two or more are gathered in His name...' Together, these angels created business opportunities, improved family relationships, a few significant relationships, joy, peace, acceptance and lots of love.

"May We Discover Together,
The Deeper Purpose of Our Relationship"

This exciting new relationship discovery book, co-authored with David A. Smith, is based on the Just Dessert Seminars complete with experiential exercises. Discover the deeper purpose in your relationship. It is about creating your own "fairy tale", discovering and owning your role, creating a space for your life partner, renewal of the spirit, intimate connection and playing in the love zone.

"Seminars and Weekend Retreats"

One day seminars and fun filled weekend retreats designed to allow you to fully experience life from a position of accepting others as well as yourself. You will experience your full potential in life and learn to recognize when you are in harmony with the world. Experiential exercises based on "May We, Discover Together, the Deeper Purpose of Our Relationship" will add new purpose to your life.

"Ice Breaking 101"
Getting to Know You in One FUN Question!

A fun, light-heart resource book for stimulating fun and connecting to people any place and any time. A teaching resource for stimulating creative thinking. Use for written, verbal discussions and art assignments. Discover the real personality with a few simple questions.

Dessert T-Shirts, Caps and Cups

Especially designed just for you and your unique dessert personality. Show the world what you are! Let them know you have been Touched~ by Perry A~.

Watch for these other Sweets... Coming Soon!

"May We Create Our Own Vows"

A sequel to "May We, Together, Discover the Deeper Purpose of Our Relationship". Renew your vows in special and creative ways. Commit to Sacred Days and times spent together. Come to the Just Dessert Seminar and create your own sacred vows at the Rainbow Connection.

Sweet Rewards Game

A board game designed to give you the experience of the benefits of team play. Experience your Sweet Rewards in a FUN Win/Win format where there are no losers. Experience Bridges to Happiness, Barriers to Happiness, Angel Thoughts and Just Dessert Personalities as you claim your Sweet Rewards on the Cherry Pie of Life. Watch out for the Sour Cherry! The game is complete and in pre-production at this time. Prototypes available for play at Seminars.

Dessert Stationery and Stickers

Send special, colorful, visual images along with your messages. Better than a quote, these are appealing and non-fattening. Add colorful stickers to envelopes, letters, books, even baby diapers (Rumper

Stickers! "My Little Strawberry Shortcake") Decorate the world with dessert images.

Dessert Cards

Pick a card from the deck and see what personality traits you will most need in your life today. Just watch your day take shape knowing ahead of time that you need to be focused, spontaneous, organized or outgoing. It is all in the cards.

For ordering any of these FUN products
or for further information, please call
1-800-50-SWEET.

~Index of Desserts~

Kiwi Fruit 37

Lady Fingers 27

Lemon Chiffon Pie with Raspberry
    Topping 47

Lemon Chiffon Soufflé, with
    Raspberry Sauce 52

Lemon Meringue Pie 47

Low Fat Yogurt 42

Marshmallow 60

Mississippi Mud Cake 27

Napoleon 60

Oatmeal Cookie 30

Oreo Cookie 31

Peach Cobbler 37

Pecan Pie 47

Pineapple 38

Pineapple Upside-Down Cake 28

Prune 38

Pumpkin Chiffon Pie 48

Raspberry 38

Sand Tart 31

Star Shaped Tea Cake 31

Strawberries Romanoff 52

Strawberry Hot Fudge Sundae 42

Strawberry, Kiwi, Mandarin Orange
    topped Cream Cheese Pie 48

Strawberry Pie 48

Strawberry Shortcake 28

Sugar Glazed Donut 60

Tapioca Pudding 52

Triple Layer Ice Cream Pie with Fudge
    Sauce 48

Vanilla Pudding 53

Vanilla Wafer 31

Whipped Cream 53

White Chocolate Mousse 53

~SWEET AFFIRMATIONS~

~Sweet Notations~

~Scrumptious Notes~

~Delicious Results~

Experience A Touch of Perry A~ With Programs From The Heart

PEOPLE ARE JUST DESSERTS . . . *Experience the Sweet Rewards.*

Create harmony in all your relationships with the Recipe for Sweet Rewards. Blend differences gently for Sweet Results. Build a Sweet Team. Dissolve resistance, eliminate justification and increase potential. People are the desserts of life. Keynote/Workshop.

OBSTATUNITIES . . . THE BRIGHT SIDE OF UNPLANNED CHANGE

Challenge change for positive results. See obstacles as opportunities for expanding your horizons. Change *your perspective* and reap GIFTS. Join Perry A~ for a look at life from another point of view. It is about saying YES to LIFE! It comes a la Cajun humor and Fun. Keynote/Workshop.

HOW TO TEACH A ROCK AND DEVELOP THE WILLINGNESS QUOTIENT

First you ask the "Rock" if they are WILLING to participate 100%. Develop harmony by eliminating justification, judgmentalness, criticism and right/wrong thinking. See one another as perfect and whole. Exchange resistance for openness. Most "Rocks" are willing to learn once they are accepted and understood. Seminar/Workshop.

OBSERVATIONS OF A SUBSTITUTE TEACHER

Learn to recognize and effectively deal with dramas. Glimpse behind the drama to understand the root cause. Re-direct this energy for positive results and have fun doing it. You don't have to be a counselor, just a little common sense will suffice. Seminar/Workshop.

Order Form
Discounts available for bulk purchases.

Item	Price	Qty	Total
"People Are Just Desserts" Book	$14.95		
"May We, Discover Together, the Deeper Purpose of Our Relationship" Couple Discovery Book	$14.95		
"Thank you for Listening But I Wasn't Quite Through!" Book of Short Stories	$11.95		
"A Touch of Daisies" Book of Affirmations	$9.95		
"Ice Breaking 101" Book	$11.95		
"People Are Just Desserts" Tape	$8.00		
Obstatunities Tape	$8.00		
A Touch of Perry A~ Tape Short Stories	$8.00		
T-Shirt - "My Sweet Rewards are on the Way" Teal/White L___XL___	$10.00		
Sub-Total			
Send check or money order to: **Perry Arledge** **Perry Productions** **P.O. Box 33512** **Austin, Texas 78764-9998** **1-800-50-SWEET** **Fax 512-441-0206**	**Texas Res.** **add 7.25% tax** **Ship Charge** **$2.00 per.** **Total**		

Credit Card Orders

Visa or MasterCard #_____ Exp. Date_____

_____
Print Name on Card & Signature (Required for Credit Card Purchases)
Send To:
Print Name_____

Address_____

City_____ State_____ Zip Code_____

Phone Number (____)_____ Please allow 2-4 weeks for delivery.